AF604549

The **Importance** of the **Environment**

Vegetation in Australia

VEGETATION IS ANOTHER name for plant life. In Australia, there are four basic vegetative regions, each with its own special plants and animals. The type of vegetation that grows in an area depends on the rocks and soil beneath, and the weather patterns above. For example, in northern Queensland, where the climate is hot and rainy, rainforest vegetation grows. A rainforest species, such as the hoop pine, couldn't survive in the outback, where it rarely rains and switches between scorching days and cold nights.

Forest

A forest consists of trees grouped closely together. The treetops touch, creating a closed canopy with plenty of shade underneath.

Leadbeater's possum: Also known as fairy possums, these tiny marsupials live in the mountain ash forests in central Victoria. They are critically endangered and fewer than 1500 individuals remain.

Leadbeater's possum

Grassland

A grassland is a flat, open area covered with grass and only the occasional tree. Sometimes they are called savannahs, especially if they are found in a tropical region.

Gouldian finch: In the tropical savannahs of northern Australia, you can find rainbow-coloured Gouldian finches munching on grass seeds with their strong beaks.

Woodland

In a woodland, the trees are spaced further apart compared to a forest. The open space between trees allows plenty of sunlight to reach the ground, meaning grasses can grow.

Northern hairy-nosed wombat: These critically endangered wombats like to dig their burrows in sandy soil near trees, because the roots give their underground homes extra stability.

Woodland

Grassland

Forest

Desert

Ancient History

Australia's vegetation has changed over time with our changing climate. About 99 million years ago, Australia was located much closer to the South Pole and was joined to the supercontinent Gondwana. Back then, it was covered with temperate forests consisting mostly of beech trees. As the Australian continent broke away and drifted north, it entered a warmer climate zone. Eucalyptus and acacia species replaced the beech forests, as they were better adapted to the strong sunlight, higher temperature, lower water supply and more frequent fires.

Did you know?

About 85 per cent of plant species in Australia are endemic – this means they aren't found anywhere else in the world!

Vegetation Transformation

When Aboriginal people settled Australia 65,000 years ago, they also changed the vegetation patterns, using fire. By burning forests, Aboriginal people promoted the formation of grasslands, which they preferred for hunting. European settlers have also altered Australia's landscape, by clearing native vegetation to raise farm animals and plant crops.

Desert

Deserts are characterised by having almost no rainfall. They often have dry, sandy or rocky soil. During the day, temperatures in a desert can be very hot, but night time in the desert can be surprisingly cold. Plants that grow in the desert are specially adapted to these harsh, dry conditions.

Sturt's desert pea: There aren't any native cacti in Aussie deserts – but there are beautiful flowers. Sturt's desert pea is the floral emblem of South Australia, but it occurs across much of Australia's arid, sandy interior.

Forests

A FOREST CONSISTS of trees grouped closely together. The treetops touch, creating a closed canopy with plenty of shade below for a multitude of species.

Australia has the seventh biggest forest area in the world, equivalent to nearly 125 million rugby fields. But not all forests are the same – they can be vastly different. In Australia, there are eight distinct varieties of forest, categorised by their main tree type: acacia, eucalypt, callitris, mangrove, casuarina, melaleuca, rainforest and 'other natives'.

Eucalypts make up three quarters of Australian forests. Because they evolved in dry conditions, eucalypts are fire-tolerant and will regenerate after being burned.

Our forests give us important resources, including honey, timber and essential oils. They are important for other animals too, providing habitat for more than 2200 vertebrate species (animals with backbones – not bugs).

▲ **Mountain ash:** Also known as swamp gums, these giant eucalypts are the second tallest tree species in the world. Australia's tallest tree is a mountain ash, called Centurion. It is found in Tasmania and measures 99.6m tall.

▼ **Golden wattle:** Famous for its bright yellow flowers, the golden wattle is our national flower. They are part of the acacia family. Acacia wood is used by Aboriginal people to make spears, clubs and hunting boomerangs.

SPECIES SPOTLIGHT

▼ **Tiger quoll:** Quolls are carnivorous marsupials about the size of a house cat. They like to live in wet forests, where they climb high into trees to hunt for birds and mammals.

▲ **Glossy black cockatoo:** These parrots prefer to hang out in the casuarina forests of eastern Australia, where they munch on the tasty casuarina seeds.

SPECIES SPOTLIGHT

Daintree rainforest

The Daintree Rainforest in tropical northern Queensland is the oldest rainforest in the world, estimated to be 180 million years old. Although it makes up only a small portion of Australia's total forest area, it hosts a remarkable diversity of life. Thirty per cent of Aussie frog, marsupial and reptile species, and 65 per cent of bat and butterfly species call the Daintree Rainforest home.

▼ **Strangler fig:** In forests, very little sunlight reaches the ground – but trees need sunlight to grow. Strangler figs have developed a sneaky way to reach the sunlight faster. Strangler fig seedlings sprout among the branches of tall trees and then grow their roots downwards, 'strangling' their host tree.

Cycads: Aboriginal people ▶ from the Daintree learned how to process the poisonous seeds of these ferns. They roast, crush and soak the seeds and roots to make a flour that is safe to eat.

Cassowary: Cassowaries ▶ are large flightless birds related to emus. They are the 'gardeners' of the Daintree: by eating and excreting rainforest fruits, they help to disperse the seeds of more than 200 rainforest plants.

Did you know?

The traditional custodians of the country around the Daintree Rainforest are the Eastern Kuku Yalanji people.

Woodlands

In a woodland, the trees are scattered further apart compared to a forest. The open space between trees allows plenty of sunlight to reach the ground, meaning grasses and shrubs can grow. Woodlands often occur in transitional areas, between the moist forests on the coasts and dry inland deserts. Most woodlands in Australia are dominated by eucalyptus species.

Australia's woodlands are an ecosystem under threat, as many have been cleared to make way for farmland. Removal of firewood also puts woodlands at risk. We might think of picking up dead sticks as 'cleaning up', but fallen branches and dead trees are an important part of the ecosystem. Old trees develop hollows that make perfect homes for parrots, possums and gliders. Branches and logs on the ground provide shelter for many reptiles and invertebrates.

▶ **Malleefowl:** These ground-dwelling birds live in the mallee woodlands of southern Australia. Instead of using a nest, they build a mound of dead leaves to keep their eggs warm. Male malleefowl tend to the mound to make sure it stays at a toasty 33°C.

◀ **Regent honeyeater:** These beautiful black and yellow birds are critically endangered. They feed on eucalypt nectar in the woodlands of south-east Australia.

SPECIES SPOTLIGHT

▲ **Honey possum:** These tiny marsupials weigh about the same as half a Tim Tam biscuit. They live in the woodlands of south-western Australia, where they slurp up nectar with their brush-tongue.

Frill-necked lizard: When ▶ disturbed, the frill-necked lizard will display its umbrella-like neck ruff. These strange reptiles can also run on two feet. They inhabit trees in the tropical woodlands of northern Australia.

Great Western Woodlands: The southwest corner of Australia is home to the largest temperate woodlands on Earth. The Great Western Woodlands cover an area bigger than England and are called a biodiversity hotspot. Scientists have found more than 3500 plant species here.

Did you know?

The yellow box gum is one of the best nectar producers in Victoria and a popular Australian honey, yellow box, is named for it.

IRONBARK WOODLANDS

IN EASTERN AUSTRALIA, box-ironbark woodlands are an important but endangered ecosystem. There are four main tree species in these woodlands: yellow box gum, white box gum, red box gum and red ironbark. Eighty-five per cent of all box-ironbark woodlands have disappeared since European settlement – in part because these trees make great firewood.

Aboriginal people have used box-ironbark woodlands for millennia. The bark of ironbark trees was used for constructing shelters, while box gums are particularly useful for building canoes and shields. The colours, carving and lines on a shield show where a person is from.

Grasslands

A grassland is a flat, open area covered with grass and only the occasional tree. Sometimes they are called savannahs, especially if they are found in a tropical region. Grasslands receive less rain than forests, but more rain than deserts. They often have cracked, dry soil in summer but can be wet and waterlogged in winter.

Grasslands around the world are under threat because they are often located where people like to have farms and towns. In Australia, there is a huge arc of tropical savannah that stretches across the northern portion of the continent. There are also grasslands in the Australian Alps, where special grasses have adapted to the cold climate, snow and dry winters.

SPECIES SPOTLIGHT

Red kangaroo: All of Australia's kangaroo species live in grasslands, where they munch on grasses. The red kangaroo is the biggest kangaroo species. It lives in the tropical savannahs of northern Australia, as well as in the desert.

Boab trees: Many grasslands are dotted with trees. In the tropical savannahs of the Kimberley, boab trees are a common sight. Boab trees have thick, bottle-shaped trunks for storing water. They can be ancient, with some trees as much as 1500 years old. They are also a staple food source for Aboriginal people – the young leaves, nuts and roots are edible.

Did you know?

Grasslands are very important to Aboriginal people in Australia. They have used a method called fire-stick farming to nurture grasslands for thousands of years. This method of controlled burning keeps areas open and grassy, perfect for hunting.

SPECIES SPOTLIGHT

Golden-shouldered parrot: These endangered parrots live in the grasslands of Cape York in northern Queensland, where they eat the seeds of firegrass. They build their nests inside termite mounds.

Striped legless lizard: This species might look like a snake, but it's actually a lizard. Through evolution, it has lost its forelegs and only has stubby protrusions where its hind legs used to be. This legless lizard lives in the grasslands of south-eastern Australia.

Flock bronzewing: Found across the Mitchell Grasslands, sometimes these pigeons gather in huge flocks of up to thousands of birds. Flock bronzewings have learnt to eat the undigested seeds in cow poo.

Julia Creek dunnart: Scientists thought that these tiny mouse-like marsupials were extinct, until some were found on the Mitchell Grasslands in 1991. They emerge at night to hunt insects and small skinks.

Mitchell Grasslands: The Mitchell Grasslands stretch across central Queensland and the lower Northern Territory. They consist of treeless plains covered with short, brown grass species called Mitchell grasses. Much of this area is used for cattle grazing, but there are some special species here too.

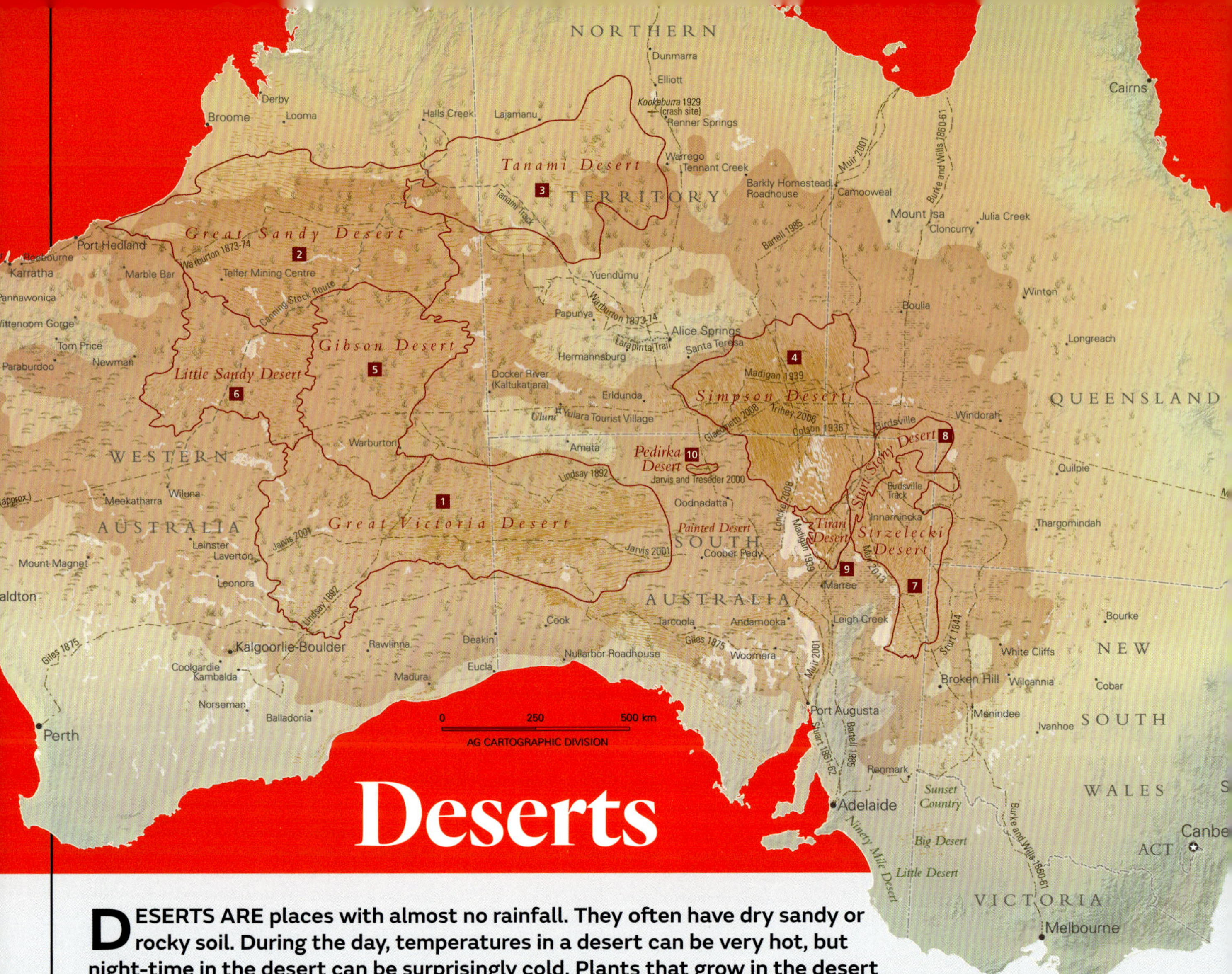

Deserts

DESERTS ARE places with almost no rainfall. They often have dry sandy or rocky soil. During the day, temperatures in a desert can be very hot, but night-time in the desert can be surprisingly cold. Plants that grow in the desert are specially adapted to these harsh, dry conditions.

There are ten deserts in Australia, and together they make up nearly one-fifth of the landmass. They receive less than 250mm of rain per year – which is actually quite a lot for a desert. The Sahara Desert in Africa only gets 10mm of rain each year. But the rainfall in Australian deserts is unpredictable. It comes in big thunderstorms and can form temporary salt lakes, which are an important oasis for many species.

1. Great Victoria Desert **(348,750sq.km)**
2. Great Sandy Desert **(267,250sq.km)**
3. Tanami Desert **(184,500sq.km)**
4. Simpson Desert **(176,500sq.km)**
5. Gibson Desert **(156,000sq.km)**
6. Little Sandy Desert **(111,500sq.km)**
7. Strzelecki Desert **(80,250sq.km)**
8. Sturt Stony Desert **(29,750sq.km)**
9. Tirari Desert **(15,250sq.km)**
10. Pedirka Desert **(1250sq.km)**

Did you know?

Not all deserts are hot and sandy! Antarctica is classified as a desert – the world's biggest – because it never rains there.

SPECIES SPOTLIGHT

Spinifex grass: These spiky tussocks are common across the red desert, and make excellent habitats for many reptiles, birds and mammals. There are 64 spinifex species across Australia, including one that tastes like salt and vinegar chips.

Thorny devil: This spiny lizard is skilled at acquiring water in the desert. At night, dewdrops form on the devil's body. Channels between its spikes carry the dewdrops to the its mouth. Thorny devils can also absorb water through their skin.

Bilby: Bilbies are like rabbits, with their big ears and burrowing habits. They have become Australia's native Easter icons – but sadly, they're endangered. The Martu people, who live in the Great Sandy Desert, are working to conserve bilbies on their country.

Kutjera/desert raisin: This desert plant is part of the tomato family. The fruit dry and shrivel on the bush, resembling raisins. They taste like strong, tangy sundried tomatoes.

Special Bulletin:

Surviving in the Desert

Over many millennia, Aboriginal people across Australia have learnt how to live in the arid Outback. Here are seven strategies for surviving in the desert:

1 **Community:** Survival in the desert means working together. Neighbours share country, knowledge and resources.

2 **Move to find water:** Water is key to desert life. People travel to use permanent and seasonal waterholes.

3 **Look for alternative water sources:** You can dig up certain roots, which can then be drained. Water-holding frogs can also be unearthed and emptied.

4 **Grinding seeds:** Some Aboriginal people are experts at using grindstones to prepare grass seeds. The ground seeds can be baked like a cake on a fire.

5 **Hunting:** Animals like kangaroos and emu can be hunted with spears or boomerangs, or caught with well-placed nets.

6 **INSECTS.** Witchety grubs are a valuable source of protein. Honey ants and the honey of native bees are good sweeteners.

7 **Follow the seasonal rhythms:** Life ebbs and flows in the desert according to rain. Using fire to manage country and roaming according to the seasons is essential.

Habitats and shelters

A HABITAT IS THE place where a particular plant or animal lives – its home. It is an environment that provides an organism with everything it needs to survive: enough food, the right climate, shelter and mates.

Forests, woodlands, grasslands and deserts are all types of habitat. There are other types, too, including cities, mountains, wetlands, and rockpools. What a habitat is like depends on the rocks and soil, the climate, availability of water, and the altitude.

Some animals can live in more than one habitat, like the Australian white ibis that lives in both cities and wetlands across Australia. Other animals have very a specific habitat, such as corroboree frogs that only live in bogs high up in the Australian Alps.

Aboriginal shelters

Many Aboriginal peoples were nomadic, travelling across country and setting up semi-permanent camps along the way. They learnt the best ways to use what was around them to construct shelters. One type of temporary shelter, much like the tents we take camping today, is called a humpy. Often, a humpy was made from large sheets of bark from paperbark trees. Some people built dome-shaped huts using saplings or cane as a frame, covered with bark, leaves, grass or earth. Some Aboriginal people also built permanent structures, such as stone huts at Lake Condah in south-west Victoria.

FINDING SHELTER

Just like humans need a house to keep us warm, dry and protected from harmful animals like mosquitoes, many animals also need shelter to stay safe and vegetation provides that.

1 Rocky outcrops: Rocks provide plenty of sunbathing spots for cold-blooded reptiles, as well as nooks to hide from predators. Rock-wallabies take advantage of the shady shelter to escape the heat on scorching days.

2 Rotten logs: Fallen, rotting wood provides food and shelter for a range of fungi, beetles and millipedes. Bigger animals use dead logs too: numbats in Western Australia need hollow logs to nest in.

3 Shelterbelts: On farms, planting strips of native trees and shrubs protects cattle, sheep and crops from strong winds while also providing shade.

4 **Tree hollows:** Around 300 native species rely on tree hollows for shelter, including parrots, frogs and possums. It takes many decades for a hole in a tree to form, which is why big old trees are important habitats for larger animals like cockatoos and owls. In many cities and towns, people construct special nest boxes to provide a home for their local wildlife.

Did you know?

The owlet nightjar is the smallest of all nocturnal birds in Australia, and also one of the most common.

Erosion and vegetation

EROSION IS A geological process where rocks and soil are worn away by the action of wind or water. The broken-down material, called sediment, is swept away to another location.

Erosion by wind ▶

Erosion by wind is a type of physical erosion. Winds can blow away loose sand, soil and dust. It can also wear away rocks, making them smaller and smoother or sculpting them into interesting shapes.

Erosion by water

Most erosion is caused by water: rivers, rainfall, floods and the ocean. The movement of the water can cause physical erosion, where rocks smash together and crumble into smaller pieces. Water can also cause chemical erosion, where the water reacts with minerals in the rocks. For example, when iron reacts with water, it breaks down and forms rust – this is a type of chemical erosion.

Erosion by ice

Moving ice can cause physical erosion by grinding against rocks. Huge rivers of ice, called glaciers, move very slowly. As the ice flows, it carves out valleys. Mainland Australia used to have glaciers during the last Ice Age, but these have since melted away. There are glaciers in New Zealand's mountains, and also on Australia's sub-Antarctic Heard and McDonald Islands.

Factors affecting erosion

1. **Climate:** **How rainy and windy a place is, and whether a place experiences extreme weather events like floods.**
2. **Topography:** **The shape of the land and how steep it is.**
3. **Vegetation:** **How much plant life covers the landscape.**

HUMAN IMPACTS & VEGETATION BENEFITS

Vegetation helps to slows down erosion. Roots hold the soil in place, meaning it can't be swept away as easily. Vegetation also shelters the soil from harsh winds, and helps the ground to soak up more rainwater like a sponge, rather than the rain washing over the soil surface.

Erosion is a natural process, but in many places, human activities have accelerated erosion to harmful levels. Clearing vegetation means that soils erode more quickly. Over time, less and less good soil remains for growing crops and pasture.

Nature's sculptures

Erosion can create beautiful natural sculptures, like the Twelve Apostles rock formation along the Great Ocean Road in Victoria. Here, the stormy Southern Ocean and big waves erode the steep limestone cliffs. This causes arches to form, which eventually collapse into free-standing pinnacles like we see today. The sea is still eating away at the rock stacks, with one collapsing in 2005.

Urban vegetation

IN CITIES, the landscape is mostly covered by buildings and paved streets. But trees, gardens and green spaces are an increasingly important part of our urban areas.

URBAN HEAT ISLANDS

The concrete we use to build our roads and buildings absorbs sunlight, and then radiates it back out into the air as heat. This makes cities hotter than surrounding rural areas by several degrees, an effect called an 'urban heat island'.

Where can we plant the vegetation?

A lot of ground-space in urban areas is dedicated to streets and buildings. But there is plenty of room on walls and roofs to create gardens!

- **The City of Sydney has more than 96,000sq.m of green walls and roofs. That's equivalent to nearly ten rugby fields.**

- Melbourne has about 100 green roofs, 50 green walls and hundreds of green building-fronts.

- **The biggest green roof in the southern hemisphere can be found in Wonthaggi near Melbourne, on top of a desalination plant.**

- Vegetation can help to cool down our cities. Plants are constantly releasing moisture through their leaves. This cools down the surrounding air – just like your body cools down when you sweat. Plus, trees provide refreshing shade.

Sustainable cities

In well-vegetated cities, people don't need to use so much air conditioning. For example, green roofs provide shade and insulation, reducing cooling costs by up to 50 per cent. In this way, urban vegetation helps us to conserve energy and be more sustainable.

Did you know?

Heat-related illnesses are on the rise, particularly impacting people who work in poorly-ventilated areas or outdoors, the elderly and infants.

Healthy humans

Urban vegetation makes people healthier and happier:

- **Plants produce oxygen and filter pollutants out of the air, improving air quality.**
- Urban green spaces reduce stress and enhance wellbeing.

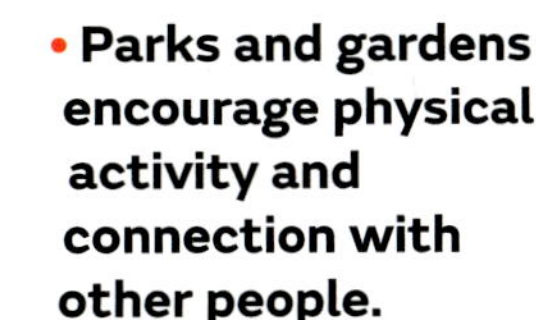

- **Parks and gardens encourage physical activity and connection with other people.**
- People who live near urban green spaces don't get sick as often.
- **Strips of trees can reduce traffic noise.**
- Vegetation beautifies our cities. It is attractive and appealing to look at.

HELPING BIODIVERSITY

Urban vegetation can provide habitat for native species. Planting green corridors throughout cities, connecting different patches of vegetation, can help prevent animals getting stuck in one small spot. Planting native species in your backyard can provide food and shelter for native animals, including pollinating species like bees and birds.

Oxygen and water

OUR VEGETATION plays important roles in both the water cycle, and in producing the oxygen that we need to breathe.

What goes in, must come out:
When it rains, water is absorbed into the soil. Plants then suck up this water, along with any dissolved nutrients, through their roots. They use the water for two different processes: photosynthesis and transpiration.

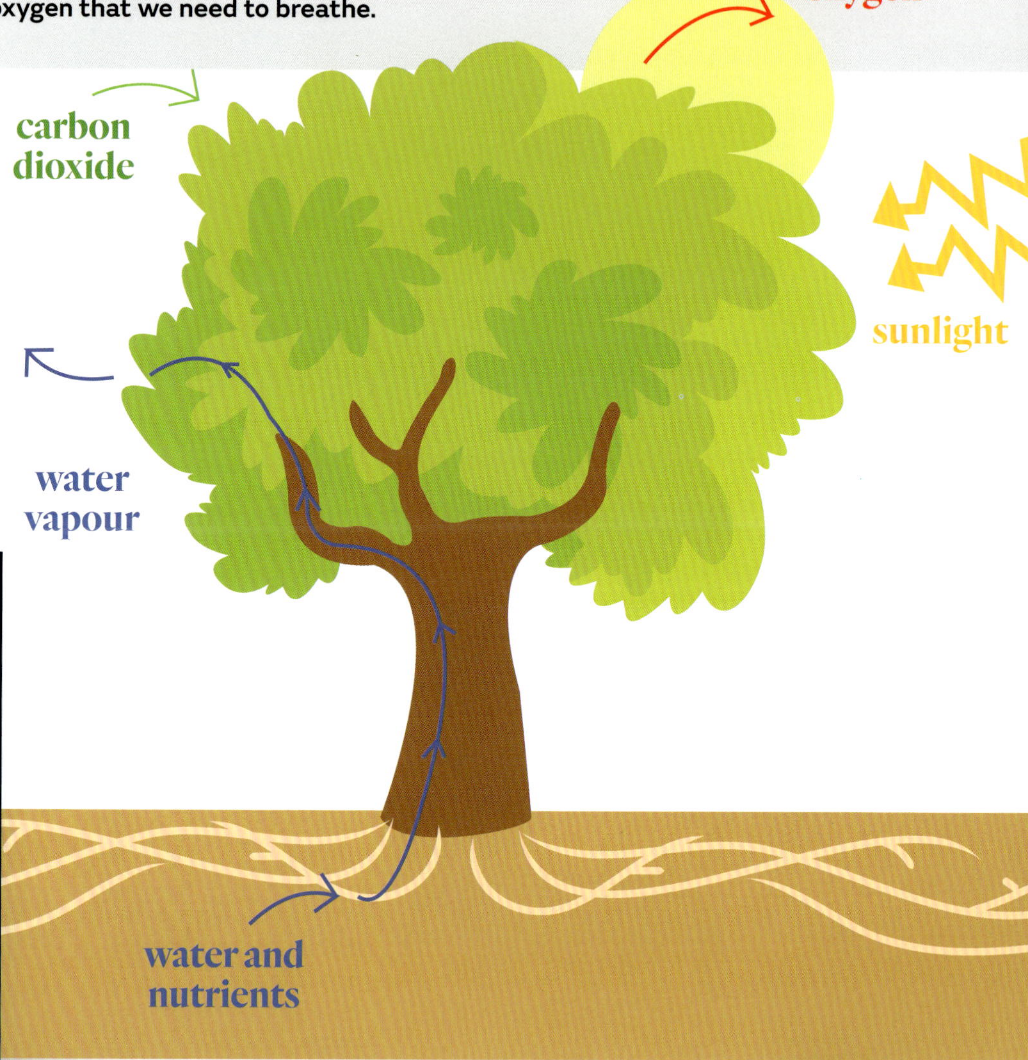

Photosynthesis

Water is an important ingredient for plant growth. Plants combine water with the carbon dioxide we exhale, and use sunlight to transform it into plant food and oxygen. This transformation process is called photosynthesis. Vegetation releases the oxygen it makes into the atmosphere – which we then breathe. About half of the Earth's oxygen is made by plants on land (the other half comes from plankton in the oceans).

The importance of vegetation

Water and oxygen are crucial for humans to survive. As our population grows and the climate warms, access to clean water and air are becoming more important topics. Australia is the driest inhabitated continent in the world, and its rainfall is highly variable. The ability of plants to store and filter water is very important. Plants also store carbon, taking it out of the atmosphere. The Earth's trees collectively take more than a hundred billion tonnes of carbon dioxide out of the atmosphere every year.

Water-saving strategies:

Vegetation grows in places where it only rains irregularly or doesn't rain much at all. So how do these plants survive without much rainfall? It turns out many of them have special adaptations to help them conserve water. For example, boab trees have bottle-shaped trunks for storing water. The leaves of eucalyptus trees hang vertically to help them stop drying out in the harsh sunlight.

Did you know?

The Amazon rainforest makes its own rain clouds by releasing water vapour through transpiration.

Transpiration

Transpiration describes how water moves through plants. Water travels up from the roots, through the stem and into the leaves and new shoots. Any nutrients dissolved in the water also get transported up to the plant's shoots to help it grow. When it reaches the leaves, water is ejected out of tiny holes as vapour (steam). This helps to cool the plant down – like the plant version of sweating. The water vapour then re-enters the water cycle, rising high in the atmosphere before condensing into rainfall.

Natural resources

HUMANS USE different parts of vegetation to make a diverse array of products.

Wood

Eucalyptus trees are cultivated in many places around the world because they are fast-growing and produce useful timber. They are the most widely planted hardwood trees in the world.

In Australia, eucalyptus wood is harvested for use in house construction, furniture manufacture, and as firewood. Eucalypts are also one of the most common sources of pulp fibre – the raw material used to make paper.

Some eucalypt species are renowned for the strength, hardness and density of their wood. Others are rot-resistant, and some are useful for building electric fences because they don't conduct electricity.

About two-thirds of Australia's log supply comes from purposefully-grown plantations. Australia's plantations, which make up just 1 per cent of forest cover, are mostly eucalypts and introduced pines.

Honey

In order to produce honey, bees need access to pollen and nectar from flowers. Several different types of vegetation are useful for beekeepers, including eucalypt forest, melaleucas (which are also called honey myrtles), Tasmanian rainforest leatherwood and native manuka.

Oils

Tea tree oil: Tea tree oil comes from the leaves of the tea tree. Tea trees are native to south-east Queensland and northern NSW.
The Bundjalung Aboriginal people crushed up tea tree leaves into a paste and applied it to wounds, as well as brewing tea using the leaves to treat sore throats. In the 1920s, scientific experiments proved that tea tree oil has antiseptic properties. Today, it is used to treat acne and athlete's foot fungus.
Eucalyptus oil: indigenous people use eucalyptus leaf infusions to treat colds, fevers and body aches. Eucalyptus oil has antibacterial properties and is often used in cough lozenges and soaps. It can also be used as an insect repellent.

ECOSYSTEM SERVICES

Some of the resources that come from vegetation cannot be bought or sold. Natural vegetation keeps our soils healthy by slowing down erosion and providing nutrients. Trees and plants also produce the oxygen that we breathe. We call these important benefits 'ecosystem services'.

Musical instruments

Aboriginal people craft musical instruments from native vegetation. Acacia, eucalypt and callitris wood is used for making clapsticks – percussion instruments for maintaining rhythm, like drumbeats. Didgeridoos are wind instruments made from eucalyptus wood that has been hollowed out by termites.

Indigenous Australians and vegetation

OVER THE THOUSANDS of years that Aboriginal people have lived in Australia, they have developed a comprehensive wisdom about native vegetation and its many uses.

Different tribes live in different areas, and so have access to different types of vegetation. They utilised the local flora for many purposes, including:

Building Shelters such as humpies/gunyahs and dome-shaped huts.

Crafting hunting equipment, like boomerangs, spears and woomera (an Aboriginal invention that uses leverage to allow a spear to be thrown up to three times further).

Bush medicine for example, tea tree paste for wounds and beach bean root extract to relieve aches and pains.

Food, such as honey and nectar for sweet drinks, fruit, and processing poisonous seeds or nuts to make them edible.

Musical instruments and toys, such as digeridoos, clapsticks, spinning tops and toy propellers.

Special Bulletin:

Aboriginal use of fungi

Over many years of experimentation, many Aboriginal people developed a 'fungal lore' – knowledge of which fungi to eat and which to avoid, and when and where to forage for fungi.

▲ Bright orange desert mushrooms were sucked on by some desert tribes as a remedy for a sore mouth or oral infections.

Stalked puffballs were used by desert peoples to hide signs of ageing. They used the powdery fungal spores to darken white hair, as well as for body painting.

Native bread is a type of forest fungus that is considered a delicacy by many Aboriginal people.

▼ Bioluminescent ghost fungi were avoided because they were accompanied by bad spirits. These fungi glow an eerie green at night, and are toxic.

Making superglue

Aboriginal people made a powerful superglue from porcupine grass and grass trees. They beat resin out of the grass, cleaned it and heated it over fire to create a sticky, black substance. This glue hardened as it cooled, and was strong enough to bind rock to wood.

Shaping the landscape with fire

When settlers arrived in Sydney, they found fields of open grass that seemed perfect for farming sheep. They didn't realise that these open parklands were actively maintained by Aboriginal people using firestick farming. This precise method of burning flushed out game animals for hunting and encouraged low-growing food plants and grassy habitat. Controlled, regular burning may also be important for avoiding big, destructive fires.

Preparing pandanus for weaving

National Reserve System

THE NATIONAL RESERVE System is an Australia-wide network of protected areas, designed to conserve our plants, animals and landscapes. Australia is a megadiverse nation, meaning it has an unusually high proportion of unique species.

OUR PROTECTED PLACE

Australia has one of the most extensive conservation estates in the world, including more than 9700 national parks, private land, reserves, World Heritage areas and other protected areas.

45%

of the National Reserve System is looked after by the federal or state/territory governments. This includes more than 7000 areas covering 8 per cent of Australia.

45%

is owned and managed by Indigenous people, representing another 8 per cent of Australia.

THERE ARE MORE THAN 1500

protected areas that are on private property, covering one per cent of Australia. In total, nearly one-fifth of Australia's land area falls under the National Reserve System.

Why do we have the NRS?

- Healthy ecosystems are essential for healthy humans. It is estimated that Australian ecosystems are worth $1.3 trillion every year. They provide ecosystem services. For example, wetlands purify the water we drink, plant life filters and oxygenates the air we breathe, and native vegetation protects against floods. The NRS is a way of looking after a diverse range of ecosystems across Australia.

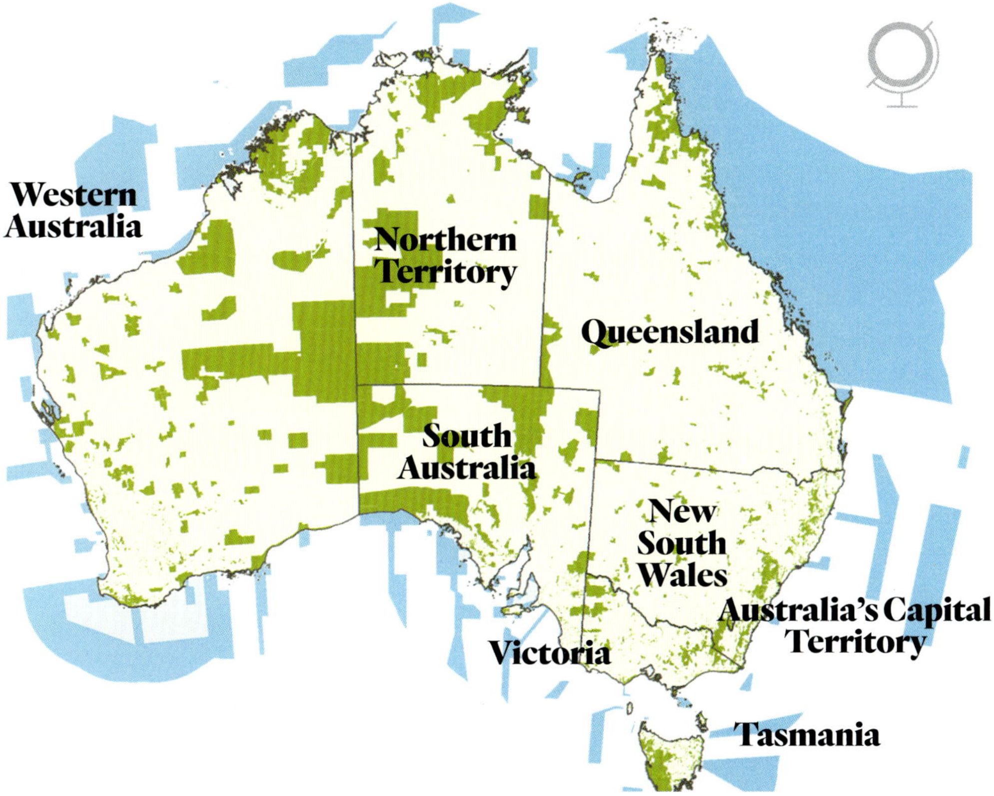

Western Australia
Northern Territory
Queensland
South Australia
New South Wales
Australia's Capital Territory
Victoria
Tasmania

Where is it?

Australia is renowned for its incredible biodiversity and range of different habitats: from deserts to rainforests. The NRS aims to include places from all the different ecosystems in Australia, so you can find protected areas all over the country.

Location of reserves in the National Reserve Systems

Protected Area

Marine Protected Area

0 250 500 1,000

Approximate kilometres

- **Many human activities, such as land clearing and farming, have altered natural ecosystems. Since Europeans arrived, these actions have led to a dramatic decline in our native species, and even extinction of some plants and animals. The NRS helps to protect habitats for native flora and fauna.**

- The NRS provides ample opportunities for people to experience different types of ecosystems through activities such as camping, bushwalking and birdwatching. Importantly, it also helps people by making jobs available, for example as tour guides and park rangers.

- **The lands protected in the National Reserve are vital in the fight against climate change. 1.5 billion tonnes of carbon (equal to 5.5 billion tonnes of carbon dioxide) is stored in the forested areas of the National Reserve System, and the ongoing rehabilitation and regeneration programs protect and can even increase our carbon stocks.**

Coastal erosion

WAVES AND CURRENTS shape Australia's coast, by pulverising rocks into sand. The ocean also eats away at the built-up sand, transporting it into the ocean and causing the shoreline to move further inland. Sandy coasts are more prone to erosion than rocky coasts.

Horsehead Rock

Changing coasts

Erosion can happen quickly during a storm or flood. Storms in 2015 and 2016 damaged beachfront homes in Sydney as waves inundated the coast, causing landslides.

It can also happen over a very long time, like the slow wearing away of the Twelve Apostles rock formation along Victoria's Great Ocean Road.

This erosion can cause problems for coastal communities, where homes and infrastructure are built close to the sea. Because 85 per cent of Australians live along the coast, it is important to protect towns and cities from erosion.

Coast guards

▶ **Mangrove forests** are like botanical bodyguards: tough, adaptable and protective. Mangroves are trees that have adapted to grow in salty water. They can help slow down coastal erosion. Mangrove forests protect the shoreline from damaging waves and storms, and catch sediment in their roots before it is carried out to sea. Australia has 41 mangrove species – more than half of all the world's species. They line more than 11,000km (or 18 per cent) of Australia's coast and cover a total area bigger than Melbourne.

Mangrove forests

▼ **Sand dunes** protect coastal buildings, houses and roads by absorbing the impact of stormy seas and big waves. In this way, they help to slow down coastal erosion. Vegetation is important for stabilising sand dunes – the roots help stop the sand from blowing away. Replanting bare dunes, and keeping off sand dune plants, are important ways to look after our natural seaside barriers.

Did you know?

Mangrove forests and wetlands are vital for the health of coral reefs like the Great Barrier Reef. They act like giant kidneys, filtering the water running off the land before it reaches the reef.

Desertification

DESERTIFICATION LITERALLY means 'turning into a desert'. It is a process where fertile but naturally dry land loses its healthy soil, water, vegetation and wildlife. Without these things, you cannot grow food crops or raise animals on the land anymore.

This type of land degradation can happen because of deforestation, drought or over-grazing by animals such as cattle and rabbits. Land that has lost its vegetation through desertification is more vulnerable to erosion and damaging dust storms.

Australia is a very dry continent. More than two-thirds of the landscape is semi-arid or arid, which means it is at risk of desertification.

Shifting sands

◀ **The Gobi Desert** stretches across southern Mongolia and north-western China. It is one of the fastest-growing deserts in the world. Each year, the desert expands south and overtakes an area of grassland equivalent to about 360,000 rugby fields. The frequency of damaging dust storms is also increasing. To stop the Gobi Desert spreading, China is planting a huge ring of forest called the Green Wall of China.

FIGHTING DESERTIFICATION

In 2017, Australia's Indigenous Protected Areas and Rangers Programmes received a Bronze 2017 Future Policy Award for their work to combat desertification. Since 1997, 70 million hectares of drylands – an area bigger than France – have been dedicated as Indigenous Protected Areas. This is the largest protected area of arid land on Earth.

More than 2600 Indigenous Rangers look after these areas. They combine western science with their own ecological knowledge to look after country. They use traditional fire management practices to save land from huge devastating bushfires. They also control invasive species and protect native species, helping to prevent land degradation.

▲ **Indigenous Protected Areas** are areas of land or sea that have been dedicated by traditional owners to conservation and sustainable resource use in agreement with the government. Traditional owners manage the land in line with World Conservation Union standards.

Protecting environments

WILDLIFE CORRIDORS are connected habitats that allow species to travel easily from one area to another. These corridors can be small pathways through local neighbourhoods or large connected habitats across different states. They are designed to protect the spaces through which different species migrate and, as temperatures rise, also provide for the change in the distribution of plants and animals that will need to relocate.

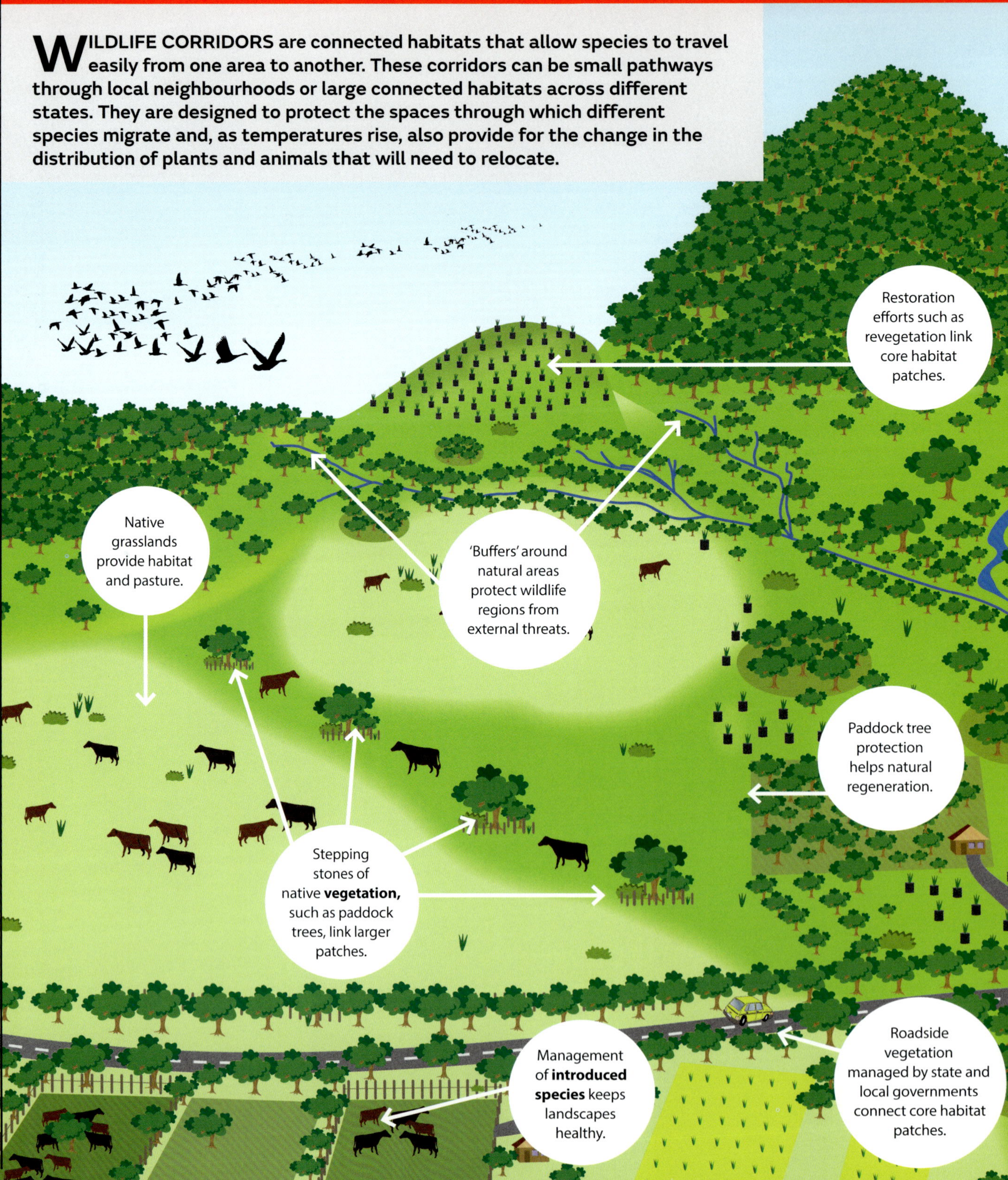

Courtesy the Department of the Environment and Energy, Australian Government

Building corridors
involves activities such as wildlife bridges across busy roads and replanting native species. Animals such as the squirrel glider have benefitted from the creation of these corridors.
Did you know?
The Great Eastern Ranges Iniative is aiming to restore a huge strip of healthy habitats across 3600km: from Far North Queensland all the way down to Western Victoria.
Large patches of native vegetation provide core habitat.
Seasonal rains trigger plant **regeneration** and provide habitat for aquatic species.
Migrating bird species rely on important wetland and shore habitats.
Suburban home owners create backyards friendly to native wildlife.

Image credits

Images are listed clockwise from top left.

Front cover: Bisams/Shutterstock (SS); Kevin Wells/SS; David Hancock/Australian Geographic (AG); Vladimir Sazonov/SS. **1:** Mike McCoy/AG. **2:** Jason Edwards/AG; Mitch Reardon/AG; Mitch Reardon/AG; Jason Edwards/AG; Jason Edwards/AG. **3:** Nick Rains/AG; Art-Pho/SS; Nick Rains/AG; Vladisvlav T. Jirousek/SS; Andrew Gregory/SS. **4:** Norman Allchin/SS; Butterflyhunter/SS; Bill Hatcher/AG; Eric Isselee/SS. **5:** Andrew Gregory/AG; Andrew Gregory/AG; Sherjaca/SS; Andrew Gregory/AG. **6:** Grenville Turner/AG; Mike McCoy/AG; Andreas Ruhz/SS. **7:** Metriognome/SS; picturepartners/SS; Jeffy Greenberg/Getty. **8:** Ashley Whitworth/SS; Mike Langford/AG; Romain Risso/Wikimedia Commons; Mitch Reardon/AG. **9:** Lauren Smith/Australian Geographic; Ryan Francis/Flickr; Chrris Steeles/Flickr. **10:** Australian Geographic Cartography. **11:** Jiri Lochman/AG; Ant Calvert/AG; Jiri Lochman/AG; Mitch Reardon/AG; Anne Hayes/AG. **12:** Jiri Lochman; Skinner Prout/Wikimedia Commons. **13:** Luke Shelley/SS; Mitch Reardon/AG. **14:** Tom Jastram/SS; Mike McCoy/AG; J. Lekavicius/SS. **15:** Alexander Vershinin/SS. **16:** Scott Hawkins/AG; STILLFX/SS; Scott Hawkins/AG. **17:** Sakaret/SS; Adam Calaitzis/SS. **18:** Designua/SS; Andrew Gregory/AG. **19:** Ajhansco/SS; I'm Friday/SS. **20:** PitchyPix/SS; Cozine/SS; Nicole Patience/SS. **21:** ChameleonsEye/SS. **22:** David Hancock/AG. **23:** Anne Powell/SS; David Hancock/AG; IMissisHope/SS; Harry Rose/Wikimedia Commons; David Hancock/AG; Petar B Photography. **24:** Bill Bachman/AG; Ronnybas Frimages/SS. **25:** David Bristow/AG; Environmental Resources Information Network/Australian Government Department of Sustainability, Environment, Water, Population and Communities; Nick Rains/AG; David Hancock/AG. **26:** Ross Tomei/SS; Faithie/SS. **27:** Andrew Gregory/AG; Leah Pirone/SS. **28:** LFRabanedo/SS; DAvid Hyde/SS; Galyna Andrushko/SS. **29:** David Hancock/AG; David Hancock/AG. **30:** Department of the Environment/Australian Government. **31:** all Esther Beaton/AG. **Back cover:** Andrew Gregory/AG

Australian Geographic

The Importance of the Environment is published by Australian Geographic.

First published in 2019

Australian Geographic
52-54 Turner Street
Redfern NSW 2016
editorial@ausgeo.com.au
www.australiangeographic.com.au

Text: Ellen Rykers and Australian Geographic contributors
Commercial Editor: Lauren Smith
Assistant Commercial Editor: Rebecca Cotton
Creative Director: Mike Ellott
Print Production: Alisha Stoddart

Australian Geographic
Managing Director: Piers Grove
Editor-in-Chief: Chrissie Goldrick
Commercial Manager: Simone Aquilina
saquilina@australiangeographic.com

The Australian Geographic Society was established to encourage the spirit of discovery and adventure, and to foster love for our natural heritage. The Society and the Australian Geographic journal sponsor scientific research and conservation, and a portion of the profits from our published products goes back into the Society. Become a member today by subscribing to the Australian Geographic journal.

Subscribe now 1300 555 176
or australiangeographic.com.au

Aboriginal and Torres Strait Islander people are advised that this book may contain images and names of people who have died.